Parenting for Academic Success

A Curriculum for Families Learning English

Unit 1:

Plan for Success

PARENT WORKBOOK

Lesson 1: Setting Goals

National Center for Family Literacy

DELTA PUBLISHING COMPANY

Copyright © 2005 by the National Center for Family Literacy

Printed in the United States of America

Parent Workbook 1   ISBN-10: 1-932748-29-6
                           ISBN-13: 978-1-932748-29-1

Acknowledgments

Parenting for Academic Success: A Curriculum for Families Learning English was developed by the National Center for Family Literacy (NCFL) in collaboration with the Center for Applied Linguistics (CAL) and K. Lynn Savage, English as a Second Language (ESL) Teacher and Training Consultant.

Principle Curriculum Authors: Janet M. Fulton (NCFL), Laura Golden (CAL), Dr. Betty Ansin Smallwood (CAL), and K. Lynn Savage, Educational Consultant.

Special thanks to the Toyota Family Literacy Program, which piloted these materials in Washington, DC; New York, NY: Providence, RI; Chicago, IL; and Los Angeles, CA.

The Verizon Foundation provided original funding for the development of this curriculum and supports the National Center for Family Literacy in its development of resources for English language learners. Verizon's support of the literacy cause includes Thinkfinity.org, a free digital learning platform that advances learning in traditional settings and beyond the classroom. Visit the Thinkfinity Literacy Network managed by the National Center for Family Literacy and ProLiteracy Worldwide on Thinkfinity.org for free online courses and resources that support literacy across the life span.

Special thanks to Jennifer McMaster (NCFL) for her editing expertise.

A Message for Parents

This program is designed for parents who want to build their English language skills. The program also will help you learn ways to help your child improve his or her skills to succeed in school.

You will do activities to learn and practice reading, writing, speaking and listening in English. These activities also share information about how children learn to speak and read English. Each lesson has an activity you can do with your child at home.

When you support your child's learning at home, your child learns how language works.

Doing family learning activities together:

▶ Helps you be your child's first teacher.

▶ Helps you learn how your child learns.

▶ Makes learning fun.

▶ Supports your child's learning outside the classroom.

You can help your child learn every day. This program will help you help your child to learn.

Un Mensaje para Padres

Este programa está creado para padres que quieren mejorar sus destrezas en inglés. A la misma vez el programa les va a ayudar apoyar el aprendizaje de sus niños y a prepararlos para tener éxito escolar cuando entran a las escuelas.

Dentro encontrarán actividades para que mejoren sus destrezas de lectura, escritura, y conversación en inglés. Las actividades van a compartir información acerca de cómo aprenden los niños a hablar y leer en inglés. Cada lección tiene actividades para hacer en casa con sus niños.

Cuando usted apoya el aprendizaje de su niño en casa, él o ella aprende como se usa el lenguaje.

Cuando hacen actividades escolares juntos:

▶ Le ayuda ser el primer maestro de su niño.

▶ Le ayuda aprender como aprende su niño.

▶ Aprendiendo conceptos es más divertido.

▶ Apoya el aprendizaje de su niño fuera del salón de clase.

Le puede ayudar a su niño diariamente. Este programa le ayuda apoyar el aprendizaje de su niño.

LESSON 1: Setting Goals

Lesson Goal

Learn about program materials and set personal educational and parenting goals.

Lesson Objectives

Today we will:

▸ Interview each other and communicate personal information.

▸ Use "wh" questions to find out information.

▸ Discuss family activities using simple present tense.

▸ Preview program materials.

▸ Identify personal learning goals for this program.

Lesson Warm–Up

1. Meet your classmates.

   ▸ Repeat the questions after your teacher.

   ▸ Read the questions below.

   ▸ Answer the questions below.

   What is your name?

   My name is _____.

   Where do you live?

   I live in _____.

   What country are you from?

   I am from _____.

   What languages do you speak?

   I speak _____ and _____.

How many children do you have?

I have _____ child.

I have _____ children.

What is the name of your child?

My child's name is _____.

What are the names of your children?

My children's names are _____.

How old are your children?

My child is _____ years old.

My children are _____ years old and _____ years old.

2. Complete the "Walk Around Interview."
  ▶ Say hello.
  ▶ Ask a question.
  ▶ Answer the question.
  ▶ Exchange cards.
  ▶ Say good–bye.
  ▶ Find another partner.
  ▶ Repeat these steps with another partner.

Points to Remember

Do family learning activities together. It will:

▶ Help you become your child's first teacher.

▶ Help you learn how your child learns.

▶ Make learning fun for both you and your child.

▶ Support your child's learning outside the classroom.

Can you add other points to this list?

_____

_____

_____

_____

3. Read and discuss the program goals.

This program will help you:

▶ Improve your English.

▶ Help your child develop his or her home language and English.

▶ Support your child's development of reading and writing skills.

▶ Understand the U.S. school system.

Can you add some other ways this program can help you?

_____

_____

_____

_____

Plan for Success

Attend every class session.
Participate in class activities.
Do Take–Home Activities with your child.
Complete Parent Surveys.

ACTIVITY 1: Key Vocabulary

Words in this lesson are listed below. Use the Key Vocabulary pages to build your vocabulary.

1. Review the words. Which ones do you know?

Word Part	Word	Example	Translation
noun	family		
noun	parent		
noun	child		
noun	children		
noun	language		
noun	country		
verb	read		
verb	write		
verb	listen		
verb	speak		

2. Practice Key Vocabulary words. Write the nouns in alphabetical order.

   Example: *child, children…*

   _____

   _____

   _____

   _____

   _____

3. Practice Key Vocabulary words. Write the verbs in alphabetical order.

   Example: *listen, read…*

   _____

   _____

   _____

   _____

   _____

4. Practice using Key Vocabulary words. Unscramble the letters to make these Key Vocabulary words.

   country   read
   family   write

   mafyli _____

   rdae _____

   teiwr _____

   trynuoc _____

ACTIVITY 2: Reading In My Family

1. Listen to the teacher read a story. Discuss the following questions.

   ▶ What is the family doing together?

   The family is _____

   _____

   _____

   _____

   _____

   _____.

   ▶ What does your family like to do together?

   My family likes to _____

   _____

   _____

   _____

   _____

   _____.

Activity 3: Scavenger Hunt

> **Scavenger Hunt**
> A game where players find answers from clues.

1. Look in the *Parent Workbooks*. Find the answers to these questions. Write your answer in the spaces below.

Where will you find:

▶ Family stories?   Unit # _____

Unit Name: _____

▶ Family recipes?   Unit # _____

Unit Name: _____

▶ Family activities?   Unit # _____

Unit Name: _____

▶ A parent–teacher meeting?   Unit # _____

Unit Name: _____

▶ Common routines to talk to your child?   Unit # _____

Unit Name: _____

▶ Songs and nursery rhymes?   Unit # _____

Unit Name: _____

▶ Story predictions (guesses)?   Unit # _____

Unit Name: _____

▶ School progress reports?   Unit # _____

Unit Name: _____

▶ Tongue twisters?   Unit # _____

Unit Name: _____

▶ Reading aloud to your child?   Unit # _____

Unit Name: _____

2. Look in the *Parent Workbook*.

    ▸ Write the unit number and title in the spaces below.

    ▸ Write the page number where you find the headings listed below.

Unit #: _____

Unit Title: _____

Lesson Goal and Objectives   Page # _____

Lesson Warm–Up   Page # _____

Points to Remember   Page # _____

Key Vocabulary   Page # _____

Learning Activities   Page # _____

Think About Today's Lesson   Page # _____

Review   Page # _____

Take–Home Activity   Page # _____

3. Do you want to know more about a unit? Answer these questions.

    ▸ One unit I want to know more about is # _____.

        Unit Title: _____

    ▸ I want to know more about this unit because _____

        _____

        _____.

    ▸ I like the _____ part of each lesson.

    ▸ I like it because _____

        _____

        _____.

ACTIVITY 4: Setting Goals

1. Think, Pair, Share.

   ▶ Think about the questions. (*Think*)

   ▶ Discuss your answers with a partner. (*Pair*)

   ▶ Share your ideas with the class. (*Share*)

   What are your dreams for your child?

   I want my child to _____

   _____

   _____

   _____.

   What do you want to be able to do?

   I want to _____

   _____

   _____

   _____.

2. Share your goals with your classmates.

ACTIVITY 5: Think About Today's Lesson

1. Reflect on what you learned. Finish the sentences.

Today I learned _____

_____

_____

_____.

I plan to _____

_____

_____

_____.

A question I still have is _____

_____

_____

_____.

2. Think about important words or ideas in this lesson.
   ▶ Read the words below.
   ▶ Discuss these words with a partner. Do you do any of these things at home with your child?
   ▶ Add new words you want to remember in the box below.

> • literacy activities
> • language development
> • family literacy activities
> •
> •
> •

3. Review the *Program Goals* and *Plan for Success* points in this lesson.

Program Goals

This program will help you:

▶ Improve your English.

▶ Help your child develop his or her home language and English.

▶ Support your child's development of reading and writing skills.

▶ Understand the U.S. school system.

Plan for Success

▶ Attend every class session.

▶ Participate in class activities.

▶ Do the Take–Home Activities with your child.

▶ Complete Parent Surveys.

List other ways you will plan for success:

- _____

- _____

- _____

4. Review the ideas in the lesson.

Lesson 1: Setting Goals

This program will help you build your English skills. It also will help you learn ways to support your child's learning and school success.

The lessons in the program and the Take–Home Activities at the end of each lesson help you use the things you learned in class with your child at home. In this lesson, you thought about goals you have for your child and identified things you want to learn for yourself.

Every lesson has the following parts:

▶ Goals and Objectives

▶ Lesson Warm–Up

▶ Points to Remember

▶ Key Vocabulary

▶ Learning Activities

▶ Think About Today's Lesson

▶ Review

▶ Parent Take–Home Activity

5. Are there other important points you learned from this lesson?

   ▶ List them below.

   ▶ Share your ideas with the class.

   _____

   _____

   _____

   _____

Take-Home Activity

LESSON 1: Setting Goals

Goal
Talk with your child about family activities.

Objectives
▸ Ask your child what family activity he or she likes.

▸ Write a sentence about the family activity your child likes.

Directions
1. Prepare. Think about the following questions.

   ▸ What family activities did you see in the *In My Family* book?

   ▸ What family activities do you like?

2. Try this at home.

   ▸ Ask your child to talk about a family activity that he or she likes.

3. Review.

   ▸ Think about the things your child talked about when you asked about family activities.

   ▸ Review the sentence examples that follow.

   Examples:
   - My child likes to play soccer with his cousins.
   - My child likes to read books at bedtime.
   - My child likes to go fishing with her father.

Useful Words and Phrases		
Verbs (present tense): • watch • play • walk	Nouns (people, places, things): • TV • books • games • soccer • church	Prepositions: • about

4. Reflect.
   Write a sentence below to tell about a family activity that your child likes.

   _____

   _____

   Prepare to share your experiences in the next class.

Actividad para realizar en el hogar

LECCIÓN 1: Aclarando metas

Meta

Conversar sobre las actividades familiares con su niño.

Objetivos

▶ Preguntarle al niño qué actividad familiar le gusta.

▶ Escribir una oración sobre la actividad familiar que le gusta al niño.

Instrucciones

1. Prepárese. Piense en las preguntas siguientes.

   ▶ ¿Qué actividades familiares vio en el libro *En mi familia*?

   ▶ ¿Qué tipo de actividades familiares le gustan?

2. Para hacer en casa.

   ▶ Pídale al niño que converse sobre la actividad familiar que le gusta.

3. Repase.

   ▶ Piense en las cosas sobre las cuales conversó su niño cuando le preguntó sobre las actividades familiares.

   ▶ Revise los ejemplos de las oraciones que siguen.

   Oraciones de ejemplo:
   - A mi niño le gusta jugar fútbol con sus primos.
   - A mi niño le gusta leer libros a la hora de dormir.
   - A mi niño le gusta irse de pesca con su padre.

Palabras y frases útiles		
Verbos (presente): • miro • juego • camino	Sustantivos (personas, lugares, cosas): • televisión • libros • juegos • fútbol • iglesia	Preposiciones: • sobre

4. Reflexione.
   Escriba una oración para contar alguna actividad familiar que le guste al niño.

   _____

   _____

   Prepárese para compartir sus experiencias en la sigiuente clase.

This survey is to evaluate the unit **Plan for Success**. There are no wrong answers and you will not be asked to talk about your answers.

1. What information did you learn from the Plan for Success unit?

   _____

   _____

   _____

2. What else would you like to know about the Plan for Success unit?

   _____

   _____

   _____

3. How will the information help you help your child?

   _____

   _____

   _____

4. Check (✔) one of the following statements about this unit.

   _____ I understood everything.

   _____ I understood most of it.

   _____ I understood some of it.

   _____ I understood a little of it.

   _____ I did not understand any of it.

   When you have finished this survey, please give it to your teacher.

Esta encuesta es para evaluar la unidad del **Plan de éxito**. No existen respuestas incorrectas y no se le pedirá que comente lo que respondió.

1. ¿Qué cosas aprendió en la unidad del Plan de éxito?

   _____

   _____

   _____

2. ¿Qué otras cosas le gustarían saber acerca de la unidad del Plan de éxito?

   _____

   _____

   _____

3. ¿De qué manera le ayudará a usted esta información para poder ayudar a su niño?

   _____

   _____

   _____

4. Marque (✔) sólo una de las siguientes afirmaciones sobre esta unidad.

   _____ Entendí todo.

   _____ Entendí la mayoría de las cosas.

   _____ Entendí algunas cosas.

   _____ Entendí un poco.

   _____ No entendí en absoluto.

   Cuando haya finalizado esta encuesta, entréguesela a su maestro.